I Know That!

Rainforest Animals

Claire Llewellyn

SEA-TO-SEA

Mankato Collingwood London

This edition first published in 2005 by
Sea-to-Sea Publications
1980 Lookout Drive
North Mankato
Minnesota 56003

ISBN 1-932889-30-2

Printed in China

Library of Congress Control Number: 2004103730

2 4 6 8 9 7 5 3

Published by arrangement with the Watts Publishing Group Ltd, London

Educational advisor: Gill Matthews, nonfiction literacy consultant and Inset trainer
Editor: Rachel Cooke
Series design: Peter Scoulding
Designer: James Marks
Acknowledgements: Karl Ammann/Ecoscene: 20. Andre Bartschi/Still Pictures: 11, 22cr. Andrew Brown/Ecoscene:
4-5, 22cl. Joel Creed/Ecoscene: 12. Digital Vision: 21. Paul Franklin/Ecoscene: 9, 15t. Michel Gunther/Still Pictures:
16. R. Andrew Odum/Still Pictures: front cover, 17t. Robert Pickett/Ecoscene: 6, 18, 23tr. Jany Sauvenet/Still
Pictures: 1, 7. Kevin Schafer/Still Pictures: 13. Roland Seitre/Still Pictures: 10. Alastair Shay/Ecoscene: 8. S. Tiwari/
Ecoscene: 14, 23bl. Patrick Vaucoulon/Still Pictures: 2, 19. Albert Visage/Still Pictures: 15b. Barrie Watts: 17b.

Contents

What are rainforests?

Rainforests are huge, very old forests. They grow in places that are hot and wet.

▶ *In the rainforest, plants grow very close together.*

4

There are many kinds of plants and animals in rainforests.

In the trees

Many different animals live in rainforests. Some of them live high up in the trees.

◄ *A spider monkey uses its tail to hold tightly to the trees.*

The branches and leaves of the trees make a roof over the rainforest. This is called the canopy.

▲ *Snakes wind their long bodies around the branches of trees.*

On the ground

Other rainforest animals live on the ground, which is covered with fallen leaves.

Leaf-cutter ants carry away the leaves to eat.

A tapir uses its long nose to look for food.

The leaves that cover the ground are called leaf litter.

In the water

There are rivers and streams in rainforests. Some animals live or feed in the water.

▼ *A capybara feeds on water plants.*

Piranhas are small, fierce fish with very sharp teeth.

The world's biggest river is in a rainforest. It is called the Amazon River.

Eating plants

Many animals eat rainforest plants. They eat leaves, flowers, and fruit.

▶ *Parrots feed on fruit. They also eat nuts and seeds.*

Gorillas feed all day on roots, stems, and leaves.

Look out for mangoes, avocados, pineapples, and bananas in the supermarket— they are all rainforest fruits.

Eating animals

Some rainforest animals are hunters.
They kill and eat other animals.

▲ *A tiger pounces on its food.*

Not all hunters are big. This hairy spider is only a little larger than the insects it hunts.

◄ *A chameleon flicks out its sticky tongue to catch insects.*

Colors in the forest

Dull colors help an animal to hide. Bright colors make sure an animal is seen!

► *Tiny plants grow on a sloth's dull coat. This makes it hard to spot.*

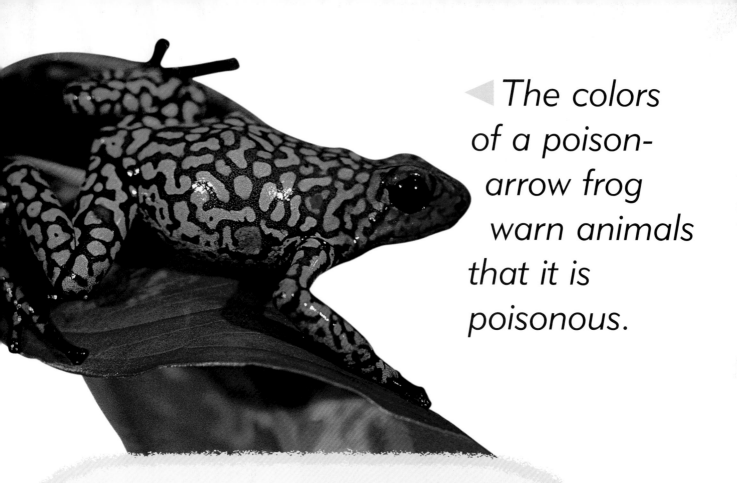

The colors of a poison-arrow frog warn animals that it is poisonous.

Like a poison-arrow frog, a ladybug's bright red color tells other animals that it is not good to eat.

Calls in the forest

Rainforests are noisy places. Animals call to one another through the trees.

◀ Monkeys how

▲ Frogs croak.

Animals in danger

Many rainforest animals are in danger. This is because people are cutting down their forest home.

◀ *The orangutan is one of the many rainforest animals in danger.*

People are trying to protect rainforests. Some parts of the forests have been made into parks. You could find out more from the WWF: www.worldwildlife.org

▲ *People cut down the forest to make new roads and farms.*

I know that...

1 Rainforests grow in warm, wet places.

2 They are home to many different animals and plants.

3 Some animals live high in the trees.

4 Some animals live in rivers or on the ground.

5 Many rainforest animals feed on plants.

6 Some animals are hunters.

7 Dull colors help rainforest animals to hide.

8 Bright colors help animals to be seen.

9 Animals call loudly to each other.

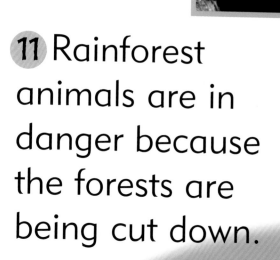

11 Rainforest animals are in danger because the forests are being cut down.

Index

About this book

I Know That! is designed to introduce children to the process of gathering information and using reference books, one of the key skills needed to begin more formal learning at school. For this reason, each book's structure reflects the information books children will use later in their learning career—with key information in the main text and additional facts and ideas in the captions. The panels give an opportunity for further activities, ideas, or discussions. The contents page and index are helpful reference guides.

The language is carefully chosen to be accessible to children just beginning to read. Illustrations support the text but also give information in their own right; active consideration and discussion of images is another key referencing skill. The main aim of the series is to build confidence—showing children how much they already know and giving them the ability to gather new information for themselves. With this in mind, the *I know that...* section at the end of the book is a simple way for children to revisit what they already know as well as what they have learned from reading the book.